THE TRAILER

THE

TRAILER

JAMES SCOLES

Clarise Foster, Editor

Signature
EDITIONS

Cover design by Doowah Design.
Photo of James Scoles by Naniece Ibrahim.

This book was printed on Ancient Forest Friendly paper.
Printed and bound in Canada by Marquis Book Printing Inc.

We acknowledge the support of The Canada Council for the Arts and the Manitoba Arts Council for our publishing program.

Library and Archives Canada Cataloguing in Publication

Title: The trailer / James Scoles.
Names: Scoles, James, 1969– author.
Description: Poems.
Identifiers: Canadiana 20210136790 | ISBN 9781773240879 (softcover)
Classification: LCC PS8637.C65 T73 2021 | DDC C811/.6—dc23

Signature Editions
P.O. Box 206, RPO Corydon, Winnipeg, Manitoba, R3M 3S7
www.signature-editions.com

For my awe-inspiring mother,
Dianne Scoles
(1941–2020)

THE INSIDE

The Trailer   13
She got my heart   19
She told me   20
She rocked my world   21
Kitchen party   22
She liked my imitations   23
Joy   24
She was my muse   25
For Rent   26
She was into my meat   27
Listed   28
She danced me sideways   29
Rise again   30
She closed our telephone   31
A single Arabian night   32

THE OUTSIDE

Small town, big shine   35
Mercy   36
She tasted beer   37
Sidewalks laced with secrets   38
Exotic   39
Little French town, southern Manitoba   40
She was like a Canadian   41
Sea of plenty   42
Mending fence   43
Lifestyles of the Contract Faculty (a vignette) 44
Irish crop failure   46
Très bien, Anaïs   47
This season's tilt   48
What the Oldest Woman in Canada Said   49
Travelling thing   50
Par Avion   51
Mind over seas   53

THE UNDERSIDE

Scar tissue   57
Currents running through   58
Flight   59
Estuary   60
Awfully becoming   61
She wasn't the best curler   62
Our yesterdays   63
Bring the Spring   64
She will always be my Valentine   65
Prayer   66
A little lost   67
She was the perfect prescription   68
love barely   69
Elegy for inspiration   70
The big miss   71
Something tender, new   72
She returned my vacuum   73

THE UPSIDE

My Baby's Waltz   77
Electricity   78
She was better at everything   79
Opportunity knocks   80
Together   81
She was great at parking   82
Mid-term   83
Sinful bit of Anaïs Nin   84
She liked my medicine   86
Just thinking of you   87
Hope   88
She was fond of my tools   89
Bishop   90
She didn't find what she was looking for   91
Epithalamium   92

Another art   93
She used to live with me   94
She left me   95

Acknowledgements   97
About the Author   99

Trailer

Noun: a mobile home, somebody who trails, especially somebody who lags behind others. Verb: to live in a trailer.

—*Oxford Dictionary*

Any given thing goes with a given environment so intimately that it is difficult to draw a clear boundary between the thing and its surroundings... the definition of a thing must include a definition of its environment.

—Alan Watts

THE INSIDE

open
the
secrets
of
our
leaky
tin
shack

THE TRAILER

I

Teaching my students the most unloved
things make for the most lovable stories
takes too much honesty: my trailer, that
perfect example, remains parked in silent

shame, like a criminal record, crouching
low in history's shadow. Nobody knows
the love given, won, made and traded be-
tween two-by-three wood-panelled walls.

I told her *the most unloved things* often *make
for the most lovable stories* that baking-hot long
August day: tilted leaky toilet, sunken floors
dark, soft, soggy in so many places. Sweet

nothings were whispered about *the economy*
and *living within our means* while she stood
tall, eyes beautiful in blue-grey sparkling
wonder under rusty windows, chubby-

bottomed old doors, pressing down; she
sank in, shook her head, but accepted my
promises. Lies. Let me open the secrets
of our leaky tin shack, show her awkward

construction, poor and painful renovations:
techniques and temper borrowed from olden
days; madness was simpler then, explainable.
By living disasters daily, the Irish learned the

hard way how to *not* bury a fighting
chance; my students learn the way well-
worn, pain-ready folks fuel top-shelf
character, how voice feeds persona.

How setting lifts the sails of a story.
And how grading gets done under
the influence of more than just
good intentions.

II

Come together it did: bit by bit,
wall after wall. Patchwork: porch,
wet sky became one for a time.
Tin begat shingle, old screws re-

birthed into galvanized. Count-
less rubbery-guck tubes made a
bit better mess of the leaky roof
edges, while inside our matchbox

true love caught fire, was every-
thing we made of every day. But
building anything unbreakable is
no easy task, especially within the

scrappy walls of a silly little dream;
it *was* all we needed, could afford,
and the love made did cover each
day's losses. Like afternoon paint

drops upon floors, thighs. Meals were
love made, mingling night-tight, evenings
rendered in cedar lust and plaster dust.
Coats of sweat, primer, passion and wait.

Stories made for another time, another
world. Alight. And why *not* betwixt thin
walls? Eleven beat-up dividers at best—
all cigarette-yellow and once-wet, some

reinforced with hopeful screws—all left
wondering what'll happen next. Waiting
to see if hope hangs on or finds a way
to fail. Waiting upon a wisdom under-

neath, the dark recesses beneath, where secrets lie buried under seven hundred square feet of domestic disturbance: a place built for the story we deserved.

III

It began in the back half, where
the floor slopes a little up our tree-
less backyard, where hot waterlines
broke the second winter. But even

the first winter was a bit broken; not
waterworks but the ridiculous fear our
love was too strong: no tin-lined walls
could ever hope to contain us. And

just like that: one by one, in quick
fashion, each appliance died. Leaks
reopened; things dug under the skirt-
ing, got beneath cinder-block footings.

Certain benefits, of course, to circling
the wagons, but the moment you move
into 1981 Slimline 54-footers certain
things are given up for other glories.

Stories cut in tin and melamine: saw-
dusty glue, sweet kitchen summer
sweats: hothouse collection of lust,
bunny dust, mouse droppings by the

frying-panful. Mealy bugs, ants watched
many lovemaking nights leave the living
room feeling oversexed, like Memory's
dirty bedroom, where loneliness nestles

in for evenings. Where bedsprings sing
sad songs: little ballads to honour such
gorgeous, creaky history. Musical charms
kept hidden. Old badges, dangerous pins.

Letters tucked into shoeboxes. Certificates
framed in K-Mart gold. Best parking spot
in the park: another thing that will not last.

She got my heart

and I got the sofa, her
dresser, the kitchen table,
two poorly-put-together
pieces of furniture. Scrabble.

All the books, mean looks;
a freezer-burnt old bottom-
feeder we meant to cook,
bake into our not-so-sodden

moments and memories;
I joked: a whole little sole
to help my broken soul heal.
One eye, big, wet and cold—

the fish's, not hers—still
follows me. It always will.

SHE TOLD ME

keep your chin up, when
she walked out. I thought
that was my best look
until I looked at myself.
I also stopped finding
money; for years I was
good at finding dimes.

SHE ROCKED MY WORLD

then rolled right over my
heart in her upbeat version
of "Steamroller Blues." But, why…
she… had… to… go: I'm certain.

I tried jazzing up June with some
"Sexual Healing" and she shook down
July in a well-orchestrated, full-album
recital of "Bat Out Of Hell." Clowning

around on *this* stage has its cost
and I guess I'll keep on paying:
our famed summer of song lost
its musical charm and the saying

now goes: she left me shaking hard as Elvis Aaron
Presley—all hips and lips—without a prescription.

KITCHEN PARTY

This glass is nearly full
of far away & fantasy.

The half-moon butterflies
its quiet light upon one

awkward truth: I can't get
away from the vivid butchery

of my need. Desire cuts from
all angles; its blade is blind.

This little ache's already
led to years of quiet bake

but only the oven seems to
know the true temperature

of my secret recipes for
delight & disaster.

SHE LIKED MY IMITATIONS

of certain classic television stars but hated some
others: my Edith Bunker bombed and Archie made
me look like a Meathead, but my George Jefferson
jumped her battery and even Mr. Cunningham had

his hardware polished. Called my J. J. *Dyno-mite*
but my Fonzie flopped faster than Gabe Kotter.
My Alf sucked but my Columbo was out of sight,
same for Radar, and cool that Kojak caught her

off guard. Not as into my Ted Knight as I'd liked
but a Jack Tripper snicker made the effort worth
it; I aimed for the stars in heaven even if my
Mork from Ork brought us right back to earth.

My acting teacher once told me my method was simply
not acting very well; I don't *own* the role. She'd agree.

JOY

A thin and desperate
sort of sleet slips over
and down the ribbed sides
of this old mobile home.

Inside, I listen to the rickety
rhythm of the weather—
mixed with the cold, wind
and wet—making love with

the leaky tin roof: a melody
to feed my hungry blues built
out of fire, filth, education and
failure. Seeking only to find

a mood that might not match
but make this climate edge a
little closer to mild. Find a
resting place for the demons,

a tidy grave for this old wintry
depression.

SHE WAS MY MUSE

until we could no longer click,
it came down to a single word
that shouldn't make one sick.
Slip into our day like a sword

it would, plunging the depths
of our togetherness: one word to
leave sweet Inspiration sweating
it out on the sideline, wondering who

killed the alphabet, the very alchemy
of our partnership. Poems lost their
lustre, fine characters fled my stories
for better settings, things to wear;

we had no chance, chalked it up to learning.
It *was* disconcerting, but for her, concerning.

FOR RENT

(after match.com)

Month-to-month,
one old heart bent
on pleasure. Pretty
clean and ready to
move on into.

As is, and all
furniture, a bit
mismatched,
ill-chosen and
dated (double-
meanings intended),
stays.

A few vices, lots
of verses. Music,
dancing, okay.

~~Best offer.~~

~~All offers accepted.~~

Please offer.

SHE WAS INTO MY MEAT

loaf but not how I spiced things up;
it was the same for my steak marinade.
For me, a little cayenne in my ketchup
works wonders; never thought we'd fade

over food. She assured me it wasn't *me*,
specifically, just one thing I cooked with.
Passion was right, temperature raised nightly;
teaspoons of touch, cupfuls of love sifted

daily. As for my marinade, and my secret
recipe for no success: curry, cinnamon, red
pepper flakes; all things she liked, even let
it sit super-long. But the one thing I added

and couldn't live without, she hated. And thus
it was that yellow mustard came between us.

LISTED

Ready for inspection,
just not too close:
leave the underside
for a rainy day &
let the water build
some more pressure
before testing the flow—
those in the upper reaches
of the trailer park haven't
completed their ablutions.

SHE DANCED ME SIDEWAYS

then waltzed out of my place
with this "Achy Breaky Heart" half-
hanging out of an old fiddle case
humming "Ashokan Farewell" for a laugh;

so went our rhumba. Our kitchen
party dance machine fell from
Solid Gold to dark-and-cold. Then
our tango morphed into a rotten

old mango the same day we found
dry rot in our foxtrot; she couldn't
quickstep fast enough away: our
cha-cha went *wah-wah*. As would

my Macarena, making her mad with slide,
hip-hop and jazz; things just didn't jive.

Rise again

Let this baking-hot
trailer be the resting
place for regret & let
the sand between my
toes live just a grain
of my dreams: to
slowly seed this
not-exactly-
beachfront
property.

SHE CLOSED OUR TELEPHONE

banking option when she ran out of PIN
codes; we knew them by the letters on our
phone. A transfer, a withdrawal (no big sin),
and what started out with LOVE soured

to LIKE. Took me some time to figure
out her system, followed by short periods
of withdrawal (nothing truly sinister);
once it was clear I'd cracked her codes

she shifted unceremoniously from
DUDE to DONT and quite quickly
to DICK; I was pretty much DONE
for. The bank called, and in a sickly

voice told me my access was declined;
she now does all of her banking online.

A SINGLE ARABIAN NIGHT

No bitter cold fronting this
feature in high definition:

simply another serious
discussion left unsaid,

swept under a snow-
white carpet stolen

from another fairy
tale's predictable

happy ending.

THE OUTSIDE

shakes
like
an
old
train
tightening
up
its
schedule

SMALL TOWN, BIG SHINE

Tough luck at this little
box office: the film has
been shredded and the
lights are dim. But see
the usher still sweeping
her light? Not looking
for rule-breakers, just
wrinkles in the dark.

MERCY

In the Age of Delirious
we drank like dandelions
helped downturn dreams
not fighting fierce enough
for the dance floor.

We forgot our manners
while dropping our banners
veil after veil until each gypsy-
kissed rambling heart lay bare.

We depended upon
elevator wine: hoped we
could bring our belows
right up, maybe even
ride level with all the
others left languishing.

But that was the
Age of Delirious.

Where in the streets
we smiled, got together
to laugh out loud, hold
hands loosely: a couple
in a crowd.

Where terrible
odds like us—a hundred
to seven, at best—tend
to settle for lives as
favourite numbers.

SHE TASTED BEER

way better than I ever could
but *Barley forward* made me
giggle and that wasn't a good
thing on our third date. We

were well into our second flight,
too, and I was happy with *Hoppy*
even cool with *Crisp notes, right?*
An orange-slice came between

us, started our *Citrusy* downfall,
and while she's still a super-fan
of micro-brews, especially ale—
Sly, bitter after-taste—a cold can

works for me. Especially a Guinness,
which, by the way, has a *Smooth finish*.

SIDEWALKS LACED WITH SECRETS

Brokenhearted feels no
different in the centre
of Winnipeg; at least

the west side offered
its solace in police cars
and domestic silence.

The wisdom of the Red
River may be a better
destination than another

woman's gaze, but that
current has never run true.
Like me its awkward course

was built for confusion, a curse
carried, borne by the architecture
of its pathway.

EXOTIC

These thighs and that mole
are making a mockery of
my progress today. One
mere pilgrim on this wee
silk's route: now caught
in a dream of basting
her edges and kissing
all curves. No grip,
just glory in the new.

Little French town, southern Manitoba

(after Rimbaud)

Trapped in a false-front firecracker
waltz, her heart hid nothing but one
silent wish: her sort of water was
always just waiting to boil over.

Hers was a low down, early-birthed
passion, crept together like squeaking,
slow-screwed wet lumber under the cloud-
shadows of Notre Dame de Lourdes. Empty &

electric, thunderbolt streets. A secret dark
forest that never flies in fall. Wee churches
busted clean of sin & hellish rains. And *Jesus*
she's happy after the storm's all done with

its fun. In a saint of a southeast wind &
beautiful on her broken bicycle. Gamboling
down my rutted lane. Singing her skirt &
wearing dirty songs. Far from the city,

a hundred miles in mystery from downtown.

She was like a Canadian

music legend: not *exactly* Murray or MacNeil
and certainly not as Sweet; more Morrissette-
like: a Jordan Twain travelling the Myles—real
sassy, too—a Platinum Blonde in "Black Velvet."

We met at the Parachute Club; it was Prism-
atic: she made me *Rise Up*; right up, up *Up!*
She was a Trooper: singing McLauchlan a little
like Luba, playing guitar in a Mahogany Rush;

I told her: I'm your Loverboy. You've got my
Streetheart. Our Harlequin romance needs the
Honeymoon Suite. She shook her head, said I
had turned into a real, true Cochrane. Hart-less,

Jagged Little Pill, eh? All because of my Great Big Sea–like mouth
our "Patio Lanterns" dimmed, and love—like a "Snowbird"—went
south.

SEA OF PLENTY

Fields like waves,
the wind white-
capping the rye.
Soy bean leaves
caught in an off-
shore breeze: green
tide feeding this
sea of plenty.

Quarter-section
away the combine
calms all leafy greens
into beds of chaff, hope
& stubble: shaving the
grace from the prairie's face.
Fitting end to a season's
worth of growth.

Sweet birdsong,
leaves lending
their wave-like
sparkle, a back-
ground to give
this afternoon
its glory. Flitting
killdeer & their
lyrics of foreshadow:
late-summer sky's
just getting ready
to pour its kind
offering into
this field's
generous
pores.

MENDING FENCE

Barbed wire cuts
tears & scars make
perfect sense today:
some retribution for
this bucketful of sins.

Dust off the tools &
toss out the rules of rough-
but-fair trade & make no
room for error: this is
serious family history.

LIFESTYLES OF THE CONTRACT FACULTY (A VIGNETTE)

Cue the loon. Hear the lilting flute.
See the shuffling, hurried feet as we
Follow the creature's uncalculated
Route down the dim-lit hallway of its
Unnatural environment: the university.

Wrinkled costuming in well-worn,
Unpolished shoes is a common
Form of the creature's mimicry,
Making it difficult to discern
One creature from another.

Habitats include basic shared caves,
Basements, closets, storage rooms and
Stairwells; spaces rather indicative of the
Creature's potential, future prospects and
Liminal nature of its existence.

Socio-agronomic studies reveal diets
Rich in little, a life low in esteem, and
A penchant for self-punishment;
Tests also reveal alarmingly
Poor taste in fashion.

Sex is regularly undermined and
Constantly undetermined due to
The creature's irregular schedule,
Ability to cower and blend, and the
Chameleonic nature of its employment.

While highly intelligent, communicative,
And the bread-and-butter of universities
Worldwide, the creatures—including
Sessionals, Adjuncts, Temps, Terms and
Turn-ups—remain socially awkward.

Approach with caution. Although
Docile in its work setting, fierce
Competition for scarce resources
Means conflict is not uncommon
Among members of the species.

Cue the loon.

Irish crop failure

Weather is leading this
charge into my future
forecast: ready to set
the barometer low
and the debt high
as it'll go—get
buried in shame
and accept the
shanty, what my
kind were called
upon arrival.

Très bien, Anaïs

Thanks for your tremble
the trance laid bare upon
my heart feeling ready.

How incredible: you looking through
the ardent train of frenzy—that saunter
of your desire—waking the seniors
for three blocks down
                              there
where I hope to travel.

You don't know what it's like yet
to be middle-aged at thirty
still chasing sleep
in the streets of your image.

Left waiting
patiently
obedient
to your religion.

THIS SEASON'S TILT

Measure this season's
tilt from rapture to
rupture—the incision
and scar still in
negotiation.

Snow is just finding
its sanctuary, its fit
and feel for a way
to bury and blanket—
even bandage—things
not quite sorted

before the Fall.

WHAT THE OLDEST WOMAN IN CANADA SAID

(upon my grandmother's 111th birthday)

If ever you happen to find
yourself under a spell—cast
or uncast—please, just accept.

Then please yourself with
more than just ideas of what
needs doing: teach your hands
so your Self can do all things.

Of the world, she said: travel
until you've seen through all
lands bathed in sand, all seas
made silent by the tides, reefs;
kiss the sandbars & shoals.

Believe in yourself, she said: leave
your foot's print only in the dark
and give wonder a push into light.

Accept each & every spell be it good
bad or ugly indeed, she said, for life is
not to be continued soon just only if.

So, she said, where steam finds you
rising and your bread baked well?
Listen.

TRAVELLING THING

The lusty old travelling thing
hasn't yet ruined to dust, hasn't
yet taken its tale to another table.

That old feeling still ruckles
and shakes like an old train
tightening up its schedule.

Steel wheels making hot love
with twin tracks, one steam-driven
beat-up dream driving the beast.

PAR AVION

We remember the special days—
her birthday, mine, when major
appliances died—love-making
mornings digging for rare desert-
diamonds; love like favourite
songs forever following you.

Images of parked cars, kissing.
The good kind of crying. The hard
missing: that perfect spectacle of
yearning. The ache cast under
heaven's watch.

Swimming in the multitude of
early miracles (sad old shoeboxes
sure love her letters). Magic languages—
sweet, naked words—never went seeking
meaning (such lyrics never fail to hit the heart).

Incredible lovers leave beautiful
things painted inside: their unique,
permanent imprint upon you. Another
body's impatient first, middle & lasting
impressions (like airmail letters from afar).

You savour each day's disaster & dance
—flirting with your world's edges—carrying
memories of a life lived outside the mailroom.
You still seek a way to better feel that slice of
life's wise history not long gone.

Something with an accent & the sea
still connected: a crinkled airmail envelope.
Its soft, thin, well-travelled blue paper.
Hand-written. Roughed up & well-
touched. Foreign, dispatched.

Still warm from travel. A
miracle sent from afar
& held onto. Kept.

Something from a lover.
From somewhere whole
worlds away & above the
ordinary. Between you &
what tore you apart: long
distance love over the seas.

MIND OVER SEAS

Give me just the crust
the remainder of what's there
the bread sweet
neat this afternoon
cold.

Swarm and spawn:
wander whole worlds while wondering
and upon sunshine
rise and find.

Towering over the purity
of our pale blue history
your outcome well within
our boundaries
border wide open
for all travellers
& devotees.

Poised before the corner-store's
refrigerator you find frost and shake
pennies from grandmothers
fallen while over knees not seas.

She asked me:
>   *What do you do?*

I said:
It's a long story.
It's better we should
>   *get us a room first.*

THE UNDERSIDE

meaty
shadows
that
hide
just
below
the
skin

Scar tissue

Open these old wounds easy
as memories—the indelicate
album of crevices I'm left to
care for—and listen to the
sea of love still spilling my
blood, playing my bones
and singing its song
of havoc so sweetly
through broken skin.

CURRENTS RUNNING THROUGH

Underneath, inside & all
over: memories are
eroding this shaky
foundation already
built upon a river
of bad concrete.

We bravely swim
the backstroke—
eyes wide open,
buttered in pain—
waffling over the
rock-hard memories
of things both
stupid & ripe.

We feel how the
current builds, toys.
How it plays. The way
it flays our histories
with gypsy-like clarity.

Even my electric train knew
nothing pretty lives
                under the stairs
or in the scars: those meaty
shadows that hide just
                below the skin.

But that's the way the
currents play. How they
flay our history with a
flare & each day strip
our hearts right bare.

FLIGHT

(after Ludvigson)

He remembers how love
left—one talon clutching
a calendar filled with
special days—simply
spread its wings
with a sigh and
then circled the
blood-red sky.

He thought it might
return—even set
some of the special
days free or teach
a few how to fly—
but love kept soaring
slowly disappearing
into that sky.

ESTUARY

Could have let the current
carry away yesterday, but
every channel of this bent
and swollen old river cuts,

captures this boat's attention.
One epic journey yearning
to yield for no creek's junction
nor lay its keel into learning

the sandbar's grip. Just how
to steer away from a new
class of rapids. But now
the anchor's hooked anew,

snagged at the delta of do something soon
or go down slowly, scuttled in the lagoon.

Awfully becoming

All that remains now
rests upon your ability
to pay debts, bills, and
penance toward levelling
the balance between
unstable ground and
a slow, steady landslide.

SHE WASN'T THE BEST CURLER

but when she was mad at me she could
curse like the greatest of all: The Wrench.
Known for not ever missing a shot—wood
toothpick forever conducting the air, clenched

in his teeth—Ed Werenich was a legend of
the game. But if he ever missed, the media made
damn sure the microphones were well above
and far from the foul-mouthed, full-on tirade

he would unleash (only on a rock or himself).
For us, it was love right out of the hack: she
was my Sandra Schmirler—a trophy shelf
full of Scotties, Briers, big-money bonspiel

wins—but when she had the hammer, she'd lay it
on the button better than *both* of Canada's greatest.

Our yesterdays

Memories of her come
out like the hot horse
from the gate, then flood
my field with hoof-prints.

Miracle odds from the start,
a tropical storm since birth:
an electric eclectic peripatetic
cloudburst, right off the hop.

A hurricane twisting through
me and our yesterdays
and todays and all
my tomorrows.

BRING THE SPRING

Baptism by choir in these
sun-melted streets, thick
slush & funk of frustrated
months caught in the mix
& mess of rediscovery &
better direction taken:
soul gathered, singing.

She will always be my Valentine

and I'll keep making new cards out of
the old ones, cutting out the best hearts
and cheesiest expressions of puppy love.
Pasting together all the pieces and parts,

hoping to put together another time,
when my little red-papered shoebox
was stuffed full of wishes and rhymes
for Valentines. Praying my hopeful slot

could manage the giant cards others got
but for me simply never came; until she
did: smiling like a secret admirer caught,
across the classroom of our love, where we

played footsie, held nervous hands and first kissed.
The cards remain to remind: how much she's missed.

PRAYER

Lightning, come strike
this craving from its perch;

let rolling thunder and sweet
electricity collide in education

and teach this little addiction
some manners; at least make

it plant its seeds of failure
further apart. Let the light

and roots raid the soil daily
for depth and spoils. Open

the heavens. Strike this steel
fear into the shape of something

better; give it the sort of
blacksmithing it deserves.

A LITTLE LOST

Happens to the worst of
us, the shiftless and the
listless. Left wandering

the old halls, searching
all walls with memories
framed in discomfort:

discounted images
tattooed upon the
skin of our hearts.

She Was the Perfect Prescription

but the pharmacy couldn't read the doctor's
handwriting. Our world caught cold, our
needs needed feeding; the doctor cocked her
hand when codeine couldn't cut it. To cure

allergies you face them head on; not this one.
Sudafed made us hungry, rest left us listless.
Pills we had were past their prime *plus* one;
I suggested a different approach, which

for months worked like a blacksmith.
Now all we do is drink and have sex, she
proclaimed. I saw no problem with
her assessment, but suggested we

consider something like therapy.
She had another idea: cold turkey.

LOVE BARELY

End of an era ushered in:
a cinema of catastrophe
bankruptcy among friends &
another circus-built freak show.

And now love barely breaks
the idiocy of the moment
the game on the television
& the scene of your x-ray.

But a closer examination won't
reveal the bones of your guilt:
that quilt knit into your skin
& very genes & the real, true

history you're responsible for.

ELEGY FOR INSPIRATION

Digging this slow-
developing grave for
rejection reminds me
of the work it takes daily
to feel the fires inside
forever dying
to ignite.

The big miss

(after Roethke)

Early on, our game got thinking:
let's play the bed like quiet pros;
such drinking never led to sinking.

Bedding for show, putting for dough:
our bodies smiled from ear to fear;
wasn't long before this game slowed.

Early games were good for the soul
and often loved to leave us sighing;
sinking was never drinking's goal.

Laughter and loss were laundered
like linen; caddies carry the crying;
was it wrong for us to be drinking?

The sky might fork its tongue of slight
while I pray our bedding wasn't lying;
who could've shot our stars from night?

Dear partner—half our twosome rendered—
our happy little life now seems squandered:
our bedding took time off for thinking
and now the drinking's only sinking me.

SOMETHING TENDER, NEW

This road's been dark
for too long: time now

to light the way with
a fire built to convey,

carry more than messages
of hope & faith, a visage

of something tender, new:
lust rekindled to keep this

fire fed for the long nights
not quite warm enough to

light the pile of yesterday.

SHE RETURNED MY VACUUM

damaged (like me) and well-
used. Broken light (it was
always a bit dim), scuffed

and scratched. Wheels that
leave tracks (like the ones
across my heart). But sad

as it was (the break-up), and
is (the vacuum), it still sucks.

THE UPSIDE

laughing
at
losing
works
for
me

MY BABY'S WALTZ

(after Roethke)

The heat from her body
Used to make me dizzy;
I hung on for dear life:
Such loving wasn't easy.

We romped frames crooked
And got the trailer rocking,
At least until our spooked
Neighbours got to knocking.

The body soldered to mine
Was made for long sessions:
We came together like sunshine
And sea in love-making lessons.

Grinder, groaner and wailer:
A world-class lover, indeed,
Who waltzed out of my trailer
And left me clinging to memories.

ELECTRICITY

Feel it singing through
the veins, touching each
white & red blood cell
with music, light & love:
a fire to remind the river
flowing, frothing from
its pulsing mouth to its
gaping delta: keep feeding
those magic fibres of muscle
forever swimming not far
from the scene of inspiration.

SHE WAS BETTER AT EVERYTHING

than me, especially a wide range of obscure,
but cool international and Olympic sports:
Dressage (never horsed around with her
fashion), Sumo (loved wee round courts

but not thongs) and Australian-rules
anything (all sorts of body contact
encouraged); very different schools
of fish were fond of her fine action

with fins and followed her Deep-Sea
Diving (especially *Into the Wreck*) and
her great skill at Jai Alai is no lie. She
made even the leprechauns of Ireland

jealous of her hurls in Hurling but in Curling her first rock
found my heart; it still lives in her house, around the clock.

OPPORTUNITY KNOCKS

Never too old to travel
these waterways &
lands that lay their
promises upon my
all-too-teaseable &
tattooed soul: baggage
always packed, ready for
rain, bog, broken road,
renegades on the run
from another wronging
& all set to knock at one
more door of wonder.

TOGETHER

(after Tretheway)

Feast of perfection found its
way into this day, a fresh
warm wind of distraction,
feeding a tide of blue eyes

made in a confusion of
moon and attraction;
a clear orchestration
tattooed in time
and transition;

discussion loves beginning
between bodies built for
these moments: a kind of
memory foam designed
for comfort *and* vision:

a simple decision made
in easy leisure for pleasure,
desire and the seizure of
all spoils of discovery

and transition
tattooed with time:
a clearly orchestrated
attraction; moon and
confusion made in

a tide of blue eyes
feeding distraction a
warm wind, a fresh
feast of perfection.

She Was Great at Parking

and could work her way into her spots
like a professional drive-instructor: each
time was an intimate interview in the lot—
betwixt vehicle and space she would reach

her goal every time, and in style—seeking
satisfaction in the sweet distance between.
Had a way of finding the right angle, peaking
her approach, and forever backing in clean.

We went bumper-to-bumper to near-fender-
bender on more than one parking occasion;
her parallel was truly unparalleled, rendering
me spent and leaving only minor abrasions.

I loved her strategy—all *feel*—and when she found the right
spot you'd know by the cry in this passenger's sigh of delight.

MID-TERM

The test being the
rest of your life
gives a little more
meaning to the best
of each day's glare—
sun protection won't
be required for this
timely dose of the
shine's share.

SINFUL BIT OF ANAÏS NIN

(after Baudelaire)

To your bible-coloured freeways
these eyes still cling, follow. Trace
the cobble of your image to
the blacksmith of your below.

In the shape of your streets—
open, rounded & loud, sexy as
Paris weather—your beauty
cries out in pure, wet perfection.

In that dark birthmark just beyond
the influence of your auburn eyes
smiling, how could I ever forget
one lone, future-fired sunset?

With you, all memories—each
flavour of your history—are as
potent as the flesh & fun, the
fantasy that love forever requests.

Let us sing this little insignia of
wax & wonder into our symbol,
a chance at some French family
history: jewels like you are so

much more valued, cradled in
less saddled-up sorts of ways &
still shining down upon my years.
For now, my only wish is to seek

your blacksmith. Steal more slowly
through your cobble. Come to know
your old town well. For your precious
image is a gift to travel (a biblical high-

way to cling to, in fact) leaving our second
song for the streets & the siren simply
waiting to wail.

SHE LIKED MY MEDICINE

cabinet more than she liked me. I'd won
it off an old, long-haul trucker in poker;
he was from California, a chain-smoker,
and it was a pharmaceutical history lesson

in a box. Bottles of white crosses, black
beauties, purple hearts and blue beans
all designed to make the miles disappear
between Barstow to Lafayette, and back.

Beauties gave her the night's sheen
while we lost our religion in the white
crosses bearing the weight of our right
pleasured, empurpled limbs; the beans

brought us back to reality, and left me alone in Lafayette.
She seems happy though, living in Barstow with the cabinet.

JUST THINKING OF YOU

reminds me of my foolish ways:
the disasters built so very well

under the bridge of tomorrow.
Not the best planning, no, but

our best suit was a birthday and
you're the only soul to make me

smile from one side of any
street to the other side of

any dance floor (reinforced
for precisely *our* sort of love)

and I keep dreaming of a roller-
rink snowball to send us so

tight together we won't
ever melt away.

HOPE

(after her)

Bit of a moon in the sky
giving light to the memory.
The what if. The what
hangs in between.

Under the influence
of her quiet, charmed
beauty made like new
music. Such tender,
sweet voices inside.

An entire season
now sings its song
of praise. Of hope.
Its song of her.

SHE WAS FOND OF MY TOOLS

but my renovations, not too
much: her taste for marble
and mayhem in the bedroom
quite often caused a squabble.

She went wild for my seamless
laminates but lost her mind over
my melamine feature wall in fish.
My plans for clawfoot and tile were

welcomed with wide-open arms
but my conversion of her home's
fireplace to gas set off every alarm.
Wasn't long before my new posters

were defaced; the nice, neat writing in her hand:
No Job Too BIG For This (*not so handy*) Handyman.

BISHOP

(after Sonnet)

Expired—a thought
bubble bursting,
electrically quieted;
the comic stripped
old and fading
derided.
Inspired—a sonnet
singing freedom,
circling high above;
no longer divided
a creature not caught;
muse praised,
a glass raised:
to Liz, with love.

SHE DIDN'T FIND WHAT SHE WAS LOOKING FOR

but she found my stolen stamp collection
when she was searching for a paper clip.
I convinced her I wasn't an aberration,
that my klepto-philately was but a slip.

I agreed that it was, in a way, cheating;
that spending time with a secret hobby
was wrong, and I quickly ended things.
Wasn't long, though, before the lobby

mailboxes were stuffed with temptation
and old habits were suddenly fighting hard
with new promises. I found my stamp collection
though; she'd kept them in a box, with her cards,

mementoes, love letters, photos from our trips—
things we'd shared—all hiding a box of paper clips.

EPITHALAMIUM

It'd be ironic to call
him peristeronic (he
pokes his little pickle
into every pigeonhole).

He was a dog-eared paper-
back to her pure hard-cover
(she peels eggplant while
he smokes Houseplant).

She volunteered sandbagging
while he was bootlegging sin
(he's the old trash in her
new blue recycling bin).

She asked for vinegar
and he spilt her wine (she
pulls him from his carapace
of lethargy, makes him shine).

She gave him muscle, hustle
hot yoga and a hash-tag (he
says: It's called an *octothorpe*;
she says: Thanks, Cro-mag).

Now, if he is me and
she is you, couldn't
all of us be true?

ANOTHER ART

(after Bishop)

Laughing at losing works for me:
why picture worry into the painting?
Keep living life longing for lovely.

Accept loss like making new love
not moving overseas on bad knees;
laughing at losing isn't all that tough.

Work to laugh better, deeper, dumber;
much better than faking your fainting:
laugh yourself into a season of summer.

Mopey-faced loser moments bumbling
like bees only mean help begging please;
laughing at losing might just be humbling.

Don't linger on disease and death, but maybe
those dentists, who are always laughing: see,
losing for them means more mad money.

Couldn't quite laugh at losing my you
when you went away from your me;
nothing's worse than missing a true.

Can't hurry the worry with a scurry
from one dream to another disaster;
certain cries you might want to hurry

just to keep crying long enough to lose
your tears, maybe a few years; then choose,
even though it might not be what you're after,
to see life with something (say it!) like laughter.

SHE USED TO LIVE WITH ME

in this trailer but not anymore; she moved in
with another man, telling me it was time to
face reality. They live in a condominium
now, and I know it isn't him *or* her who's

writing poetry, trying to process things in verse.
I tried the hard sell: At least we're not all *attached*
in the trailer park. Can't hear *every* neighbour curse.
I can hitch this sucker up; I'm not the worst catch.

Saw her the other day; she's in a bungalow
now, and just as I was saying that *I* won't be
getting water in my basement she swung low,
got the last say, reminding me: Baby, reality

is realty when your upstairs is outside
and your downstairs is the under-side.

She left me

a buck-seventy—seven coins
in the sofa (she was always
going on about *change*)—
and two mismatched
little socks that still
carry the shape of
her footprints that
walk my memory.

Acknowledgements

The Trailer is dedicated to the Scoles family: especially my mother, Dianne, who encouraged me to read & write & explore & persist, & my father, Ted, who instilled in me the never-quit fighting spirit of our Irish ancestors, & my brothers & sisters, who worked hard to keep me out of trouble & always keep me smiling: Ernie, Donna, John, Patricia & Steve.

Special thanks to: my editor Clarise Foster & my publisher Karen Haughian & everyone at Signature Editions, all of my students, current & past, all of my teachers, everyone in the English Department at the University of Winnipeg, CBC Radio & the CBC Literary Prizes, The Banff Centre, Sue Goyette (& *Ocean*), Anne Michaels, Al Purdy, David Bergen, Bill Gaston & the Winnipeg & Manitoba Arts Councils & the Canada Council for the Arts for their generous support over the years.

Extra special thanks to: Lisa Zachanowich, Tim Shea & my friends at Southern Illinois University in Carbondale, Amanda & everyone at Cousins, Times Change(d) High & Lonesome Club, The Nook, The Toad, The Road, Dennis & my neighbours & everyone at Lakeway Mobile Home Park, friends in northern & southern Manitoba, Winnipeg, Pender Island & Vernon, BC, Scoles Family Farm, Clearwater Lake, the Grassy River, The Kingfisher (Dublin), my favourite snug at Tigh Neactains (Galway), Gary & everyone at Alexander's Beach Pub (Coldstream, BC), Carolyne for her care of The Trailer, beautiful Kalamalka Lake & Kal Beach, amazing Grace (Australia), Bethany & all the dancers, dreamers, trailers & travellers of the world.

And thanks to *you*, dear reader. Cheers—*slainte*—to everyone.

Earlier versions of several poems appeared in the following literary journals & magazines: "Scar tissue"—*CV2*—Winter 2020; "She got my heart"—*The Malahat Review*—Fall 2019; "Sidewalks laced with secrets"—*Prairie Fire*—Winter 2015; "The Trailer"—e*nRoute Magazine* & CBCBooks.ca—2013; "Mind over seas"—*Descant*—2010; "Très bien, Anaïs"—*Carousel*—2005.

About the Author

James Scoles holds degrees from Arizona State, North Dakota & Southern Illinois Universities & he has lived, travelled and worked in over 90 countries. His poem "The Trailer" won the 2013 CBC Poetry Prize and his short stories are featured in *Coming Attractions 13* (Oberon Press). His writing has been nominated for The Journey Prize, the Pushcart Prize and both the Western & National Magazine Awards. He lives in Winnipeg, where he teaches creative writing and literature at the University of Winnipeg & also helps run a small, 120-year-old family farm.

Eco-Audit
Printing this book using Rolland Enviro100 Book
instead of virgin fibres paper saved the following resources:

Trees	Electricity	Water	Air Emissions
2	3GJ	$1m^3$	123kg